After London Transport METROLINE

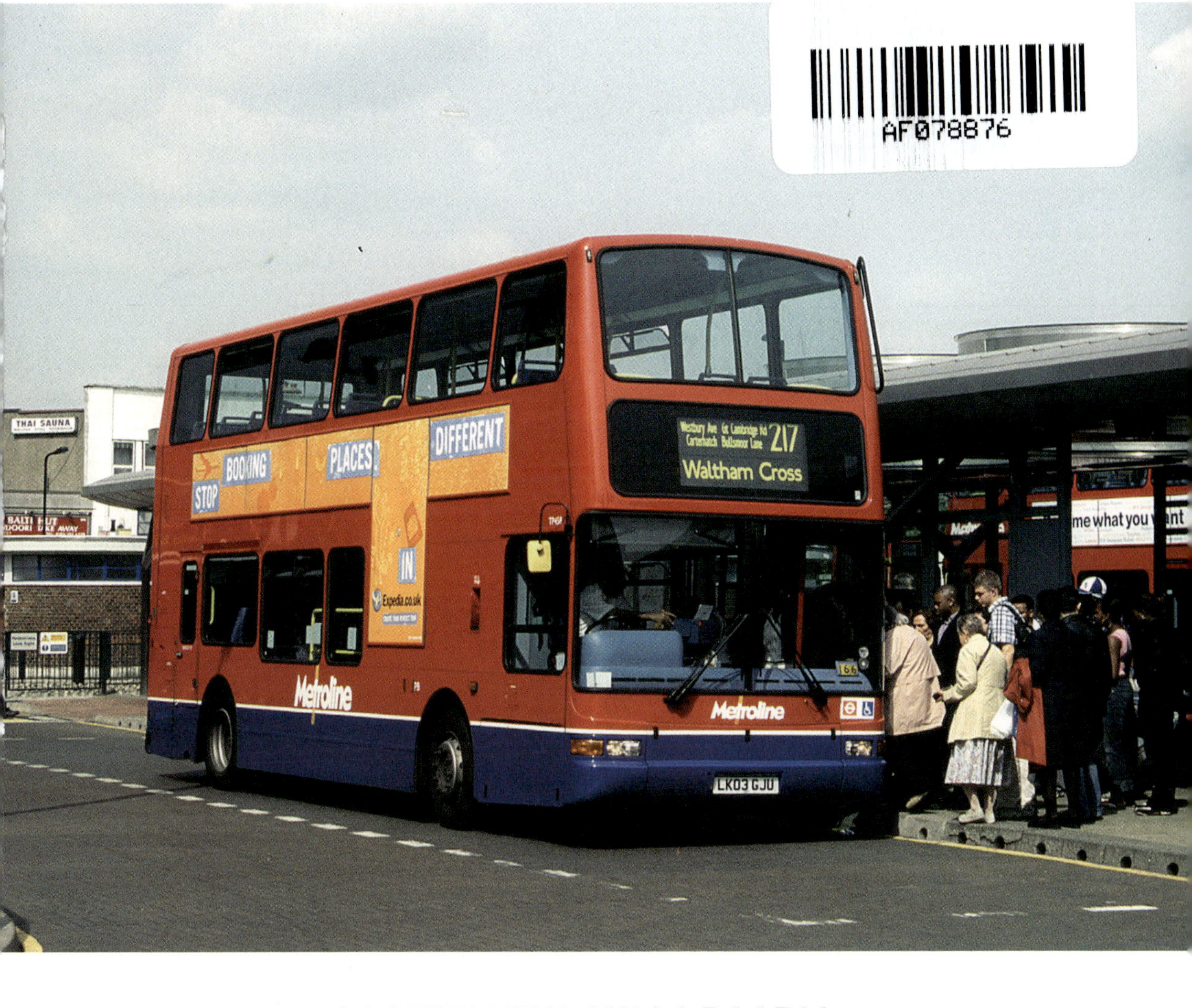

MATTHEW WHARMBY

KEY Books

TRANSPORT SYSTEMS SERIES, VOLUME 11

Front cover: In the relatively short spell between privatisation of the London Buses Ltd subsidiaries in 1994 and the later Transport for London (TfL) mandate to extinguish all livery embellishments over and above all-over red, Metroline maintained a colourful image that was characterised by its deep blue skirt. The livery, recognisably 'London' but unique enough for easy identification amid a sea of competitors, was one of many designed by Best Impressions in this period. Its base could be improved upon for specific purposes, as in the *'future...'* appellation devised for the company's first low-floor double-deckers. Alexander ALX400-bodied Dennis Trident **TA 98** (T198 CLO) was new to Harrow Weald garage for the 140 and 182 in the autumn of 1999, and on 5 March 2000 is seen at Harrow & Wealdstone station.

Back cover: The modern face of Metroline is the ubiquitous BYD D8UR-DD electric double-decker with Alexander Dennis's Enviro400City bodywork. Though a serious competitor is starting to garner orders with Metroline in the shape of the British-built (and owned!) Wrightbus Streetdeck Electroliner, for some years the Chinese giant had it all its own way. From the first batch, taken for Holloway's route 43 in 2019, is **BDE 2629** (LJ19 CVC), seen on 16 August 2019 rounding a much-recast Highbury Corner, which is no longer a roundabout.

Title page: Metroline made sure that its strict delivery times for the assumption of contracts were maintained by dividing its loyalties between Dennis Tridents and Volvo B7TLs during the rise of first-generation low-floor double-deck buses at the turn of the century. New in 2003 for the 217 and 231 from Potters Bar garage is Plaxton President-bodied Dennis Trident **TP 458** (LJ03 GJU), seen at Turnpike Lane on 25 April 2004. Dennis Dart SLFs inherited from MTL London had been in charge for the previous five years, but these buses, bought when the only low-floor buses available were single-deckers, couldn't fully accommodate the passenger loads on these relatively busy routes.

Opposite: The long march to electric double-deckers as the 2010s segued into the 2020s would seem to have been sewn up by Chinese manufacturer BYD, with Wrightbus mired in family affairs that had shaken that company apart and Volvo bringing up the rear, not for the first time. Metroline also dabbled in Optare's early electric double-deck offering but found it wanting, not least when it came to having them delivered on time. After two batches of ADL Enviro400City-bodied BYD D8UR-DDs, Metroline ordered integral Wrightbus Streetdeck EVs once this company had got back on its feet, and the first examples of the resulting WDE class entered service on Edgware garage's route 204 in the summer of 2023. Not far from its home on 6 July of that year is **WDE 2775** (LV23 DHC).

Key Books
an imprint of Key Publishing Ltd.
PO Box 100
Stamford
Lincs PE9 1XQ

Copyright © Matthew Wharmby, 2024

ISBN 978 1 80282 944 0

All rights reserved. Reproduction in whole or in part in any form whatsoever or by any means is strictly prohibited without the prior permission of the Publisher.

www.keypublishing.com

Typeset by Matthew Wharmby

Contents

Introduction 4

Chapter 1 To Privatisation and Beyond 5

Chapter 2 The Old Order Disappears 12

Chapter 3 Consolidation 44

Chapter 4 Expanding West 58

Chapter 5 Discarding Diesel 82

Chapter 6 The Future 95

Introduction

The bus-operating structure of London Transport (LT) changed repeatedly in the 1970s and 1980s as the nature of the body's ownership came under question. Having already come under the authority of the Greater London Council (GLC) on New Year's Day 1970, LT further divided its bus operations in 1979, forming eight districts in order to take better control of reliability. These were rationalised to six in 1982. In 1984 came the transfer of LT to state operation as London Regional Transport (LRT), and a year later again came the legal separation of the bus-operating arm as London Buses Ltd (LBL).

Buffeted on all sides since 1985 by competitive tendering, LBL shrank steadily. With deregulation still very much on the cards, it then divided its operations into a dozen wholly-owned units, which would shortly gain their own trading names. Assuming control of their own ordering policy, they would be competing with other LBL subsidiaries for route contracts, as well as with the private sector. Metroline, carved out of the northwestern half of the former Cardinal District and set going on 5 December 1988, was Unit no 7.

Metroline operated in a broad swathe of north-west London, its chosen name evoking the Metro-Land appellation of the suburbs that sprang up alongside the Metropolitan Railway (later part of the Metropolitan Line). Most of its fleet comprised MCW Metrobuses, with a smattering of Routemasters, and it operated out of Willesden (AC), Edgware (EW), Harrow Weald (HD), North Wembley (NW) and Cricklewood (W) garages.

My thanks go to the publishers for their faith in what will be the first of a series of books exploring the quarter-century of each major group that has arisen out of the ashes of the old London Transport.

Matthew Wharmby
Walton-on-Thames, October 2023

Symbolically taking the London Buses Ltd (LBL) identity and ethos into the distance in Portman Street on 6 June 1995 is Northern Counties-bodied Dennis Lance LN 14 (K314 YJA) of Cricklewood garage. Without the overbearing hand of the old management obliging its subsidiaries to take buses that really didn't work in London conditions (the balance of this class already having been moved off their other original route, the 302, for being too long), Metroline soon discarded these vehicles, which achieved just four years in service.

Chapter 1
To Privatisation and Beyond

The five years between Metroline's creation and its privatisation unfolded under comparatively straitened circumstances, although the subsidiary played its part in LBL's overall purchase and allocation of large numbers of minibuses. Particularly popular were Dennis Darts; members of the 8.5m DT class with Carlyle bodywork entered service in 1990–91 at Willesden and North Wembley, followed in 1992–93 by Plaxton-bodied DRs and 9m DRLs. Metrobus numbers held level, even though the Mark 2 variants used by the Harrow Buses tendered operation were returned off lease when that arm was decimated upon retendering. As for the trusty Routemasters, these were re-engined with Cummins units at the end of the 1980s and then took their place in line for refurbishment in accordance with all those owned by LBL, being treated by Mainline (formerly South Yorkshire's Transport) between 1992 and 1994.

LBL's falling under the spell of full-sized single-deckers in 1992–93 saw its Metroline subsidiary take 31 of the Northern Counties Paladin-bodied variety of the Dennis Lance (LN class) before it was discovered the hard way that they were too long for their intended deployments. Later in 1993, Metroline was included in three allocations for the first low-floor full-sized single-deck buses (the LLW class of Wright Pathfinder-bodied Dennis Lance SLFs), which entered service in 1994.

Towards the end of 1994, the subsidiary developed a new private-hire arm known as Metroline Travel, intended to carry the company's banner forward after privatisation, which took place on 7 October with the sale of 363 buses to a management buyout.

Metroline inherited over 170 MCW Metrobuses upon privatisation, by far the majority of the fleet, but most of them were over a decade old and some were in their mid-teens. Until financial stability could be ensured, either on the company's own or by seeking a buyout, the M class would have to hold the fort on its own. Cricklewood's M 84 (WYW 84T) was a typical example from the higher end of the age spectrum, new in July 1979 and finding its way to this end of the network at the end of 1987. It is looking tired in this 6 June 1995 shot in Oxford Street, but would have to wait another year for a repaint. It lasted in service until March 1999, latterly at Edgware.

After London Transport – Metroline

The 183 was a long suburban service linking Golders Green and Pinner, operating Metrobuses from Harrow Weald garage. Seen at Golders Green on 8 November 1995 is M 1047 (A747 THV), still in LBL tapegrey but without the signature roundel. A sticker from an old ticketing experiment is worn on the front.

In lieu of a full repaint, the grey skirts were often gone over first, as it was a nuisance to need two colours to touch up the wings, buses' most frequently damaged sections. Willesden's M 87 (WYW 87T) is laying over at Brent Cross on 21 July 1995.

The Dennis Dart revolution had been enthusiastically embraced by Metroline as an LBL subsidiary, with a large number of the Carlyle-bodied DT class. Willesden's DT 95 (H95 MOB), now without a grey skirt, is at the 226's Golders Green stand on 27 July 1995, not long before this route was taken over by Centrewest.

Third of the three routes chosen to pioneer low-floor Dennis Lance SLFs was the 186 out of Harrow Weald. Wrightbus Pathfinder 320-bodied LLW 33 (L39 WLH), seen at the route's Brent Cross terminus on 21 July 1995, remained in use on this route for over a decade, spearheading the rise of accessible buses in London.

After London Transport – Metroline

In the first year after its privatisation, Metroline engaged Best Impressions to design a new livery that both retained the company's identity as a red London bus operator and gave it some distinctiveness as well. Three colours of skirts were thus applied to three Metrobuses and put out in service to see what people thought. The green variant with yellow tape divider is seen on Harrow Weald's M 1035 (A735 THV) at Golders Green on 27 July 1995.

As well as green and maroon (on M 326), there was also a blue skirt, which was the one that ultimately found favour. Accordingly, the two now non-standard schemes were the first to be gone over, with Willesden's M 326 (EYE 326V) having exchanged its maroon skirt for a blue one. The 98, operated by Willesden garage since its introduction in 1992, was RML-operated on weekdays but OPO M on Sundays, as in this 23 July 1995 shot at Holborn, Red Lion Square.

Metroline lost no time in expanding, moving on Atlas Bus, a small competitor in its geographic midst. Also an ex-LBL constituent, then known as London Coaches and privatised in 1992, this firm had acquired a large number of second-hand Leyland Titans for the takeover of the 52 at the end of 1993, but this route was now once more Metroline's responsibility, even though the Titans stayed put in the short term, continuing to operate out of a base in Harlesden. Seen at Willesden garage on 15 October 1995 is T 343 (KYV 343X).

Most ex-LBL companies established coaching and private-hire arms, with an eye to securing contracts wherever they could be found. One kind of customer that dabbled a lot in this sort of thing was supermarkets, and Safeway engaged Metroline to provide free services to their large outlet at Brent Cross. Thus has Optare StarRider-bodied Mercedes-Benz 811D SR 8 (F908 YWY) been repainted in a livery to match, and on 8 November 1995 it is seen within walking distance of its target outlet.

The constituent companies of LBL had actually been entrusted with their own vehicle ordering policy ever since their establishment in 1989, but when the centre disappeared, so did the common numbering system, resulting in a plethora of class codes. A sizeable number of 9.8m Plaxton Pointer-bodied Dennis Darts new in 1996 included EDR 29 (P305 MLD), seen near its Edgware garage home on 28 September 1997. At this point no attempt was made to book registrations that matched fleetnumbers, but the practice was subsequently resumed for ease of recognition.

Metroline's first new double-deckers post-privatisation were 22 Alexander R-bodied Volvo Olympians, which ejected the 52's Titans. These too had a batch of registrations that was applied as closely as they could match the new AV class's stock numbers; this one, based at Willesden and seen at Victoria on a sunny 18 September 1997, is AV 9 (P479 MBY). The rise of low-floor buses, however, meant that this bus and others like it would have a sharply curtailed service career in the capital.

Lasting long enough with Metroline to gain the new company livery (which flatters it), but not much longer, Dennis Lance LN 12 (K312 YJA) is reposing at the 113's Oxford Circus stand on 17 September 1997. A month later, Metrobuses would return to this route and the LNs would be withdrawn, although it took almost as long as they had been in service to find buyers for the class!

No bus is more synonymous with London than the AEC Routemaster, and Metroline inherited several dozen for central routes 6 and 98, based at Willesden. Something a bit more subtle was needed to promote Metroline's identity here, which is shown on RML 2299 (CUV 299C) at Queen's Park on 3 October 1997.

Dennis's development of the industry-saving Dart into the Dart SLF proved even more successful, and over 3,000 of the type served in London. Metroline began with Plaxton Pointer bodies on two lengths, with the longer variety exemplified at Northolt on 17 November 1997 by North Wembley's DL 19 (R119 RLY).

Chapter 2
The Old Order Disappears

Independence was good for Metroline by comparison with some ex-LBL companies; expansion was embarked upon early (Atlas in 1995 and MTL London in 1998), and gradually, the purchase of new vehicles began to replace the ageing inheritance. Dennis Darts were soon followed by the new SLF variety, large batches of which extended accessibility farther and farther afield. In double-deck terms, two batches of Volvo Olympians gave way to new low-floor double-deck designs unveiled in 1999, and Metroline alternated thereafter between Dennis's Trident and Volvo's B7TL. Once enough of these had seen off the MCW Metrobus fleet by 2004, TfL (as the operating authority was now known) controversially mandated the replacement of the remaining Routemasters, which in Metroline's case was implemented on 4 September of the same year.

Contrary to the equalising ethos of competition, big corporate groups arose rapidly, and much of the ownership of London's buses has moved offshore. Delgro, the holding company of Singapore Bus Services, bought Metroline in 2000 and then merged with Comfort to form ComfortDelgro. However, the owners have remained remarkably hands-off, by contrast with corporate practice elsewhere.

Representing the 9.2m variety of Dennis Dart SLF with Plaxton Pointer bodywork is North Wembley's DLS 1 (P101 OLX) at Kilburn Park on 29 March 1998. Towards the end of their careers, this batch of seven would be renumbered DLSs 101-107, filling a gap that had since cropped up in the series.

The PR2 had received its own batch of Dennis Darts and was still running them by 1998, though their initial livery with the sponsorship details that had accompanied this route had now given way to Metroline's new livery. It looks good on North Wembley-based DR 144 (K244 PAG), seen at Wembley Park on 20 June 1998.

The Old Order Disappears

Metroline continued its expansionary streak, acquiring the operations of neighbouring MTL London on 3 July 1998. New earlier in the year for the 234 at Potters Bar garage, but also able to turn out on that route's 326 in lieu of one of its scheduled Mercedes-Benz 811D minibuses, Marshall-bodied Dennis Dart SLF DMS 8 (R708 MEW) is laying over at Barnet, Spires on 16 August.

MTL London's acquisition (as Metroline London Northern) increased the already sizeable number of MCW Metrobuses in the fleet. This one had actually been sold by LBL in 1993 but brought back to the capital by MTL two years later, the giveaway being the style of reflective numberplate used by Merseybus, the constituent part of MTL Trust Holdings. Now past its 20th birthday and looking tired for it, Holloway's M 37 (WYW 37T) is at Golders Green on 30 August 1999, operating the Sunday OPO roster of otherwise RML-operated trunk route 13.

Before coming under Metroline, MTL had been on an acquisition trail of its own, scooping up R&I in 1995 and continuing its numbering series for buses operated out of North Acton garage. MM 270 (P470 JEG) is a Marshall-bodied MAN 11.220 taken for the 79 in 1996, and on 2 August 1998 is seen in Wembley.

MTL London had been responsible for one of the most significant changes in recent years, the OPO conversion of RM-operated route 139 on 28 March 1998. Though the Marshall-bodied Dart SLFs used were manifestly unsuited to busy central London, their low-floor configuration ticked a myriad of boxes and single-deckers were all that was yet available in this form. When acquired by Metroline, they just needed the addition of blue skirts, as on North Acton's DML 15 (R695 MEW) in Oxford Street on 29 October 1998.

A second batch of Alexander R-bodied Volvo Olympians was taken in 1998 against the contract for the 16, by default Metroline's flagship route. Displayed at Showbus in Duxford on 27 September before going into traffic at Cricklewood, AV 36 (S136 RLE) has had a company plaque specially made up for the front, but this won't be carried into service as it obscures the air intake. The 16 would receive two more generations of new buses in the space of two years; these AVs would go on to spend the rest of their short lifespan on second-tier services.

The Old Order Disappears

MTL London had followed the 139's dual-doored DMLs with a batch of single-deck examples for the 217 and 231. Now in Metroline livery in this Turnpike Lane shot of 7 November 1998, Potters Bar's DML 520 (R620 VEG) has also had its original fleet number increased by 500 to denote the batch's single-door configuration.

Its fleetnumber still in MTL London's font but now carrying a blue skirt to signify its new life as a Metroline London Northern bus, DML 33 (R863 MCE) was one of a batch of Marshall-bodied Dart SLFs new to the C11, then based at Holloway garage. It is on stand at Archway on 15 August 1998.

Metroline's own preference to body Dart SLFs was Plaxton, and subsequent orders for both constituent companies were for the dual-doored DLD class. Until low-floor double-deckers were developed (which was coming), many routes in 1998 assumed low-floor operation at the price of losing their upper deck, which for a busy route like the 302, was an ordeal for passengers. On the outer edge of Wembley on 15 April 1999 is Willesden's DLD 71 (R171 VLA).

Three last DMLs furnished route 317 at the end of March 1999. Just having pulled into that route's Waltham Cross bus station terminus on 6 April of that year is Potters's Bar's DML 534 (T64 KLD), second of the trio.

Inevitably, when companies come together, vehicles begin being pooled, and no better indicator of Metroline's hegemony was apparent than the blue-skirt repaint applied to MCW Metrobus M 1234 (B234 WUL), seen coming up to Highbury Corner on 22 March 1999. The 271 had been regained from London Suburban Buses, another MTL operation, and put back into its traditional Holloway garage home.

The Old Order Disappears

Above: The '*future...*', as emblazoned on the side of Holloway's TP 45 (T145 CLO) at Bank on 20 August 1999 was in these low-floor Dennis Tridents, 65 of which took over the 43, 134 and 17 over 1999.

Above right: Volvo Olympian AV 9 (P489 MBY) was already at Willesden when the 260 was converted from M soon after being taken over from Armchair, and on 9 August 1999 is seen at Golders Green.

Visiting the 183 at Golders Green on 31 July 1999 is Harrow Weald's Dennis Lance SLF LLW 27 (L27 WLH).

Another supermarket contract operated by Metroline Contract Services was for Safeway, entrusted to DT 88 (H588 MOC) in a white livery. On 22 September 1999 this Dennis Dart is seen in the vicinity of the Camden branch in question.

Another busy route that shouldn't have had to lose its double-deckers, the 232 began a new contract with Metroline London Northern on 31 July 1999 and was converted from M to Dennis Dart SLF. On the first day of such operation, Potters Bar's DLD 117 (T47 KLD) stands at Wood Green.

Introduced in 1987, the H15 was a minibus route that accompanied the H14 up from Harrow bus station and then made a hook round Harrow Weald to terminate at Oxhey Lane. With the service changes of 4 September 1999 it was withdrawn, but is preserved for posterity by this shot of Dennis Dart DR 17 (H117 THE) at the Harrow end on 23 August.

The DRs displaced from Harrow Weald made their way across the intra-Metroline barrier to Potters Bar garage, where they replaced Mercedes-Benz 811D (MW) minibuses on the 383 and W4. Serving Barnet on 20 January 1999 is DR 16 (H116 THE).

Participating in the 'Passright' experiment, by which holders of passes were trusted to board buses on routes 271 and W7 without having to show them, are Vs 216 and 208 (L216 TWM, L208 SKD), two Volvo Olympians new to London Suburban Buses but now seen at Muswell Hill on 5 April 1999.

Metroline London Northern's 65 TP-class Dennis Tridents had been ordered by MTL London, but Metroline proper plumped for Alexander's ALX400 body when it came to specifying its own new examples for the 140 and 182 in the autumn of 1999. Showing off the central staircase specified on London's earliest low-floor double-deckers is TA 82 (T182 CLO), leaving Harrow bus station on 23 August.

TPs 1-65 came in three waves, though by the time they were all delivered they mixed indiscriminately on the 17, 43 and 134 out of Holloway garage. Later examples, like TP 37 (T137 CLO) at Archway on 21 March 2000, had one-piece upper-deck front windscreens and red roof domes (rather than black).

Central London route 10 had been OPO on Sundays since its introduction, with each garage that operated it hoping to be able to find enough buses spare from reduced Sunday allocations on their other routes. Thus did the 10 exchange its Ms for Dennis Tridents like TP 54 (V754 HBY), seen at Archway on 1 October 2000.

Furnishing the 10's Sunday OPO runout was one thing, but the 13 was a problem. Sovereign, its normal operator, was too small to be able to spare enough OPO buses on Sundays from its own 114 and 292, so the schedule on this day was transferred to Metroline London Northern from 4 March 2000. Even then, Holloway struggled, so it was further reallocated to Edgware. Unfortunately for PR, the latter had no low-floor double-deckers yet, so trusty Metrobuses had to replace the new TPs. Seen at Oxford Circus on 2 April 2000 is M 1186 (B186 WUL).

Metroline developed a habit of reallocating its routes wholesale when capacity at garages fluctuated. The move of the 232 from Potters Bar to Cricklewood early in 2000 did not include its newish DLDs, which instead turned up on Holloway's 143, as DLD 117 (T47 KLD) is doing in this Archway shot of 21 March 2000. However, the batch now running the 232 was not fitted with wheelchair ramps, upsetting passengers who had become used to them, so this batch (which was) was switched back before long.

Exemplifying the brief spell that the 232 spent with older Dart SLFs is Cricklewood's DLD 23 (R123 RLY), entering the route's turning point at Wood Green on 25 March 2000. Eventually all Dart SLFs were retrofitted with wheelchair ramps.

New Dart SLFs took over the C2 to fulfil its retained Metroline London Northern contract in 1999, and on 30 January 2000 Holloway's DLD 149 (W149 ULR) is seen at the Oxford Circus end of the route.

Metroline's original nine EDR-class Dennis Darts left Edgware and gathered at Potters Bar for the takeover of the W9 from First Capital in 2000. Pulling into the route's Southgate stand on 8 April of that year is EDR 8 (M108 BLE).

Even as they aged into their third decade, the trusty Metrobus fleet still provided valuable use as stopgaps for route takeovers if their intended new vehicles were late or existing ones were unavailable. On 26 August 2000 at Ealing Broadway M 403 (GYE 403W) is two weeks into Cricklewood's operation of the 112, ex-North Acton. Dennis Darts were being readied for this route.

The H2 and its irregular adjunct H3 could not field anything larger than minibuses, and those used were occasionally allowed to wander to the 268, a busier route also operated by North Acton. A one-off new bus for the H2 was Marshall-bodied Mercedes-Benz 811D MMS 269 (N161 YEG), which in this Golders Green shot of 29 October 2000 has been treated to a Metroline blue skirt. The H2 and H3, not to mention the 268 itself, would be reallocated numerous times over the next five years as one garage after another was closed and replaced.

The flow of Metrobuses between Metroline and Metroline London Northern now became two-way and ramped up. The 266, now reallocated to Harlesden garage when extra space was needed at Cricklewood following the closure of North Acton, is fielding M 829 (OJD 829Y) in this Hammersmith shot of 29 October 2000. It is still in the all-red of MTL London, with no fleetnames, and would be withdrawn the following April, some time after the 266's conversion to AV-class Volvo Olympians.

The minibus routes at Potters Bar received one cascaded generation after another at the turn of the century, going from MRL to MW (1998), DR (2000) and then to DRL, exemplified at Wood Green by DRL 26 (K826 NKH) on 15 October 2000. Though the W4's age profile was thus kept more or less under control, TfL accepted Arriva London North's bid to run the route with new buses the next time it was tendered.

Mindful of the very low capacity of the early low-floor double-deckers, companies investigated the 10.5m versions of all three chassis then on offer. Metroline took a batch of long-wheelbase Volvo B7TLs for the 4 and 271's contracts, though these were switched to the more important 43 when they entered service. Plaxton President-bodied VPL 159 (X659 LLX) of Holloway is seen at the Angel on 19 May 2001.

At the other end of the length spectrum, Dennis now offered an 8.5m Dart SLF. Two took over the out-county PB1 from Potters Bar, and one of them is DLM 150 (X667 LLX) at Potters Bar station on 21 July 2001.

The Old Order Disappears

Three batches of DLDs received in the summer of 2001 allocated their blocks of registration numbers haphazardly, with few matching fleetnumbers, but after 1 September's change of system, none of them would match at all. DLD 169 (Y669 NLO) was new to Holloway for the 274, and on 15 August is seen at the Angel, Islington.

The 268, by now operated from Potters Bar, was upgraded to DLD operation in 2001. Just arriving at this route's Golders Green terminus on 28 July is DLD 176 (Y153 NLK).

The 95 out of Harlesden was the third route that summer to receive new Dart SLFs. On 28 July 2001 DLD 188 (Y248 NLK) is making the right turn into Greenford Broadway.

After London Transport – Metroline

Still going as the new century commenced were the indomitable Routemasters on the 6 and 98 out of Willesden garage. Faith in the type was shown by the restoration of the original registration to the company's oldest example, RML 893 (WLT 893, ex-KFF 276, ex-WLT 893) after its valuable dateless mark had spent several years squatting on a Metrobus. It is seen at Holborn on 4 June 2001.

Further Plaxton President-bodied 10.5m Volvo B7TLs took over the 52, 82 and 113 over the course of 2001. Calling at Golders Green on 28 July is Potters Bar's brand new VPL 201 (Y201 NLK).

Already bedded in on the 52 at Willesden, Volvo B7TL VPL 169 (Y169 NLK) is undertaking a Carnival-only short-working of the route between Notting Hill Gate and Victoria on 26 August 2001, hence the blinds with only two via points.

DLDs were due to come to Edgware just as soon as they could be displaced from elsewhere, but on 25 August 2001 in its home region, EDR 10 (P305 MLD) is not immediately threatened. It would stay put until the end of 2003.

Metrobus withdrawals had quickened since the advent of low-floor double-deckers, but there was life in the old dogs yet. M 455 (GYE 455W), last in service at Harlesden, has been put to work as a staff rest room positioned at North Finchley, and is seen there on 7 July 2001.

Having specified long-wheelbase Volvo B7TLs, Metroline now did the same on Dennis Tridents, producing the TPL class. Their increased capacity was ideal for the extremely busy 140 in replacement of TAs, and on 10 February 2002 Harrow Weald's TPL 241 (LN51 KXU), with a new letter-based registration number, is at South Harrow.

The TAs displaced from the 140 took over the 263 as a regained Metroline contract. Calling at North Finchley on 2 March 2002 is TA 104 (T204 CLO), now based at Potters Bar.

When the C2 was double-decked, its DLDs headed up to Edgware for EDR replacement, with ten new examples joining them. This is where DLD 136 (W136 ULR) is seen on 18 August 2002.

As part of a renewed Metroline contract applying from 27 April 2002, the 204 was converted to double-deck operation with VPLs. Owing to the fact that its operating garage, North Wembley, could not accommodate double-deckers, the vehicles were physically based at Edgware and maintained there. Here at Burnt Oak on 18 August 2002 is VPL 210 (Y143 NLK), displaced from Potters Bar by a new TPL and still carrying its codes.

2002 was HM The Queen's Golden Jubilee, and fifty buses from across the pantheon of London bus operators were treated to gold vinyl, with paint across the tricky bits. The effect is uneven, however, as proven by Willesden's AEC Routemaster RML 2431 (JJD 431D) at Charing Cross on 25 April.

Holloway garage's open day on 22 June 2002 saw two of the company's Golden Jubilee buses displayed. Both belonging to this garage but taking the day off are Volvo B7TL VPL 163 (Y163 NLK) and AEC Routemaster RML 2620 (NML 620E), while further along is the London Transport Museum's RT 4712 (NXP 997), which made visits to several routes during the year.

The Old Order Disappears

Another cascade from an earlier generation is DP 275 (P675 MLE), one of four Darts taken by MTL London in 1997 and since displaced from Holloway to this most outer of routes operated by Potters Bar. On 21 July 2001 it is seen swinging into Potters Bar station, and on its way back will have to traverse open country to reach Greater London again.

One of two Optare MetroRiders bought in 1998 to boost the W4, MRL 223 (P448 SWX) was by this 18 August 2002 Golders Green shot allocated to Harlesden. It would move with the route to North Wembley in the middle of 2003, and again the following year, to Perivale.

Iconic for its unique status of never having been physically changed since its introduction in 1912, the 24 was, however, difficult to run efficiently and tendering would see it passed around regularly. After 14 years with Grey-Green (latterly part of Arriva), it was won by Metroline London Northern in 2002 and allocated to Holloway with new Volvo B7TLs, this time the shorter variant. Here in Camden on 7 April 2003 is VP 330 (LR52 BNE).

Sporting the highest ever number on a Routemaster-operated central London service was the 390, introduced at the start of 2003 after a late change of plans meant that the 10 assumed OPO instead. RMLs 2296 (CUV 296C) and 2310 (CUV 310C) are crossing the Holloway Road on 15 April 2003.

Now that low-floor double-deckers were standard, the 139 and 189 in Oxford Street could take new examples when their contracts were renewed. TPs were chosen for this task, with additional members of the large order put into Holloway. Here at North Finchley on 15 June 2003 is TP 348 (LR52 KVM).

Accordingly bringing the upper deck back to the 139 is TP 365 (LR52 KWG) of Cricklewood. The route had been usefully extended to Waterloo in the interim and Charing Cross, on the new section, is where the bus is seen on 14 June 2003, but the manufacturers of the blinds mistakenly printed 'South End Green' as the qualifier for the 139's northern terminus, when it should be 'West End Green', so the incorrect lines have been blacked out.

On 8 April 2003 DL 15 (R115 RLY) is seen on the eastern fringes of Camden, having taken over the 46 from its previous MM-class MANs. It is the property of Park Royal garage, formerly known as Harlesden but renamed to something with a more salubrious reputation in order not to put off applicants.

Coming to the end of their long, long lifespan, the MCW Metrobuses still at Metroline existed only as spares and extras by 2003, other than at Potters Bar, where TfL's dead hand was less of a factor. At Waltham Cross on 29 July, TP 430 (LK03 GFV), one of the Dennis Tridents new to the 217 and 231 that year, is joined by M 1111 (B111 WUL).

After London Transport – Metroline

The 260 was kept hold of by Metroline in 2003, but at the price of being sheared in half to offset the pressure of traffic. It was put back into Willesden and before long, new Volvo B7TLs took over. VP 482 (LK03 GLZ) is encountered mid-route near its garage on 20 August 2003.

The northern section took the number 460 and remained with Park Royal (ex-Harlesden), which had been designated a Trident-operating garage. Seen at Golders Green on 28 June 2003, the new route's first day, is TP 457 (LK03 GJG).

The W8 was won back by Potters Bar for Metroline, but a piece of silliness where the letter of the law was concerned prohibited its new Dennis Tridents, of the same body, length and travelling height as First Capital's outgoing examples, from taking over until the road under Edmonton Green station bridge had some layers shaved off its asphalt. Until then, DLDs were requisitioned from the 297, which put its intended TPs into service. On 29 July 2003 DLD 65 (R165 VLA) is seen in the bus station at Edmonton Green.

Photographed if just for the splendour of St Pancras station as a backdrop, Holloway's DNL 114 (L114 HHV) is on the 214 on the morning of 5 May 2003. These Northern Counties Paladin-bodied Dennis Darts had been the C2's dedicated buses in the dying days of LBL, but had since moved on to the 214 and were now eyeing their backs nervously, with full low-floor operation mandated and approaching.

The W9's EDRs were replaced by scraping together stray Dart SLFs of various bodies and lengths. With the 317 lost to Arriva London North, DML 535 (T65 KLD) held in place at Potters Bar and on 28 June 2003 is captured at Southgate.

At the very close of Metroline Metrobus operation for TfL, Harrow Weald's M 1034 (A734 THV) is coming up to Harrow bus station on 6 March 2004, with just days left in service. Two months shy of its 20th birthday, it looks all of its years, with just one opening upper-deck front window, no foglights and its body pitted with scars, but no replacement built thereafter would manage anything close to this type's legendary longevity.

Routemaster RML 2537 (JJD 537D) is even older, at 38 years of age, but 26 March 2004 was its last day, with the one-manning of the 6 and 98 looming. It is beside one of its VP replacements in Willesden garage.

26 March 2004 saw the usual plethora of special guest vehicles added to commemorate the withdrawal of Routemasters from the 6 and 98. Two of Metroline's own heritage vehicles, seen in Willesden that morning, are AEC Routemaster coach RMC 1513 (513 CLT) and MCW Metrobus M 1 (THX 101S), which had become a trainer as far back as 1992 but remained on the books for private hire and special purposes, none of which was more poignant than today.

70 Volvo B7TLs were now the 6 and 98's complement from 27 March 2004, but only a decade and a half would be got out of them. Laying over at Oxford Circus at 9 April, having been turned short of Aldwych, are two of the new buses, led by Willesden's VP 549 (LK04 CVL).

Metroline did not take any articulated buses during the period that this format was in vogue, so sidestepped the problems associated with them. In fact, the company magnanimously helped out its neighbour, First London, when its own Citaros had to be whisked off the road following a spate of engine fires, and on 25 March 2004 at Euston has put Volvo B7TL VPL 187 (Y187 NLK) into service on the 18. This bus was usually one of the 52's complement out of Willesden.

The 6 and 98 were core Metroline's last Routemaster services, but Metroline London Northern still held the 390 and its own last day of crew operation was 3 September 2004. Several weeks earlier, on 26 June, RML 2603 (NML 603E), latterly allocated to King's Cross, is setting off from Archway.

The 390 merited the longest low-floor double-deckers on offer, and took a large batch of 10.5m Volvo B7TLs. With a blue skirt reduced in depth by order of TfL is King's Cross's VPL 595 (LK04 NNO), crossing Oxford Circus on 6 September 2004 ahead of another ex-Routemaster route one-manned earlier that year.

Withdrawn at the end of 2002 after a 17-year career, most of which was spent at Willesden, M 1349 (C349 BUV) was sold to Ensignbus and used at Routemaster 50 on 24/25 July 2004 to show off how a fallen bus could be righted using inflatable airbags. The straps employed as part of this process have not been kind to the bodywork, mangling the roof line!

Undeniably weird-looking, but making up for it with the spirited performance of the Volvo B10M chassis underneath the 1992-vintage double-deck body retrofitted to this former Grey-Green coach, VE 171 (B871 XYR) was just some of the flotsam that came across when Metroline acquired Thorpes, which had bought this bus from Arriva for schools use. During the time when just about every firm within a spit of London put out every type of bus imaginable on Underground replacements, it is serving Golders Green on 29 August 2004.

Dual- or multi-sourcing may ensure timely delivery, but it prohibits any notion of standardisation, and Metroline thus had to shuffle its types around as frequently as it did its garage allocations. Having replaced its TAs with TPLs, Harrow Weald now took more VPs than it needed for the acquired H12 to at least make a run at holding just one type, even if it did mean the busy 140 had to suffer a capacity drop. Here at Harrow bus station on 18 September 2004 is VP 612 (LK04 UWU).

Now old enough for a repaint, Holloway's TP 27 (T127 KLD) is at Archway on 12 February 2005. The skirt is lower than hitherto, and that would soon be proscribed altogether. DDA-satisfying blinds have also been retrofitted, showing just two lines of via points and thus unfortunately exposing some of the next panel along.

Volvo Olympian V 202 (L202 SKD), still holding out on Holloway's 4 as the deadline for the end of step-entrance bus operation approaches, is in disgraceful condition in this Waterloo shot of 21 April 2005. Its number blinds are so shredded that not even a generous application of gaffer tape can save them!

Roadworks in Brockley Hill, north of Edgware, at the beginning of 2005, obliged the 107 to divert away, so a temporary 107B was mounted to fill the gap. Here at Edgware station on 27 March is DLD 138 (W138 ULR), which has just come up from the garage adjacent to the bus station.

Another wholesale reallocation of existing resources in 2005 jumbled up Thorpes and Metroline buses. The former, acquired in 2004, was beginning to take on Metroline's identity without yet discarding its fleetname, so before long there was the sight of combinations like MLF 122 (AJ02 ZRY), a unique one-off Marshall-bodied Dart SLF now running a route transferred to the Thorpes depot at Perivale West. This bus caught fire on 20 August 2009 while working a C11 (another route moved out of Cricklewood) and was destroyed.

When Transbus united the resources of Alexander and Plaxton (later consolidating as Alexander Dennis), production of the President body was terminated, meaning that Metroline had to return to ordering TAs after several years of TPs. The Tridents taken for the 266 in 2005 ended up being the last of that type, and on 21 May TA 652 (LK05 GGY) of Cricklewood garage is at Golders Green after a cloudburst.

After London Transport – Metroline

The last Plaxton President body sat atop Volvo B7TL VPL 637 (LK54 FWT), new to Holloway and seen leaving London Bridge on 30 April 2005.

AVs displaced from the 266 by the new TAs at the end of May 2005 moved to the 4 at Holloway to see off the worn-out Vs, but they were still step-entrance so the clock was ticking on them too. Passing through Barbican on a dull 28 November is AV 11 (P491 MBY).

Needing minibus-size vehicles for the H2's next Metroline contract, Metroline took the newly introduced Slimline version of the established Optare Solo. Perivale's NSM 662 (YK05 CCJ) at Golders Green on 2 July 2005 also shows that the numbering system has been changed so that every batch, irrespective of type, now continues on from its predecessor.

The Old Order Disappears

Every Notting Hill Carnival sees the 316 operated with double-decks, and in 2005 the batch of Tridents just deployed to the 266 at Cricklewood made their debut. Harrow Road is the location for TA 638 (LK05 GFO) on 28 August. The route really needs to be double-deck, but then and now, any thoughts of achieving this have been vetoed by locals at the southernmost end of the route.

With time running out before the TfL-imposed cutoff for step-entrance buses at the end of 2005, Metroline didn't have enough low-floor buses to comply with this diktat, though it was awaiting new DLDs for the 214. In their absence, similar Dart SLFs were hired from London United, and one of them was new to Sovereign. SDP 539 (V539 JBH) is on attachment to King's Cross in this 21 January 2006 picture taken at Hampstead Heath.

Likewise, the 4 was still using its AVs as 2005 ticked down, so Metroline hired Tridents from First to cover for them until new deliveries of Enviro400s could displace similar buses. TN 32978 (X978 HLT) was also used to cover the 214 until the hired London United DPSs and SDP arrived, and on 23 December is seen in Tufnell Park. The 214 also cried out for the capacity that double-decks could bring, but was thwarted in this aim by the residents of Highgate West Hill at the top end of the route.

Chapter 3
Consolidation

With the London Transport legacy now fully overwritten, Metroline could chart its own path within the bounds imposed by being a TfL contractor. The company had already developed a strategy of dual-sourcing vehicles, much as LT had done, and made sure that its intended types would be reliable in the long term before committing itself to any one type, hence the dabbling with MAN single-deck chassis and Scania double-deckers before going on to take as standard large numbers of Alexander Dennis Enviro400 double-deckers, plus Volvo B9TLs when this type was developed.

Across the pantheon of TfL contractors, Metroline fitted its buses with the most useful iBus command and control system over 2008, while the mid-life refurbishment became standard practice so that operators had vehicles in suitable condition for bidding to retain existing routes or going after new ones. On the down side, TfL instructed that all firms drop their livery embellishments, meaning a plain all-red livery for everyone. Where Metroline was concerned, its characteristic blue skirt was briefly turned to a brighter shade before beginning to disappear altogether.

Heralding the second generation of low-floor double-deck buses was the Alexander Dennis Enviro400, combining the best aspects of the old Alexander ALX400 and Plaxton President bodies on a reworked Trident chassis. A low point was the dumbed-down blinds, an accessibility-motivated change that was actually less helpful, by removing via points still needed by passengers. Try not to think about the ghastly pastel skirt, a stylistic goof that was quickly countermanded. This is Holloway's TE 681 (LK55 KKP), coming up to Warren Street on 12 March 2006.

The sky-blue skirt might have worked in sunny Singapore, but in London it just looked awful and its application was stopped after two batches of new buses and a handful of routine repaints. On 30 September 2006 at Camden DLD 173 (Y673 NLO), sporting a replacement numberplate with 50mm-wide letters, has been done up to match its 55-reg compatriots that had recently taken over the 214.

The most important change of 2006 was the deletion of Armchair and Thorpes as self-standing identities, with all buses now Metroline and soon repainted accordingly. Armchair's own double-deck fleet included a DT class of Alexander ALX400-bodied Dennis Tridents, one of which, DT 21 (KN52 NEY), is seen at Gunnersbury on 3 June 2006.

Armchair had adapted its livery as time went on and TfL veered towards a red-based identity; its original orange was subsumed in 2001 into this still attractive scheme that on 10 November 2006 was being carried through Richmond by Dart SLF DP 1009 (RL51 DOA). The 493 had been taken over on a temporary basis after the crumbling of Centra, the second in succession of two poor-quality operators. Metroline didn't hold on to it when it was retendered, however.

With a very rare Thorpes logo in the Metroline style inaugurated by Best Impressions is Optare Solo OSL 1 (YJ51 JWZ), taking a Mobility Bus route 972 journey out of Edgware bus station on 31 August 2006. This network of accessible routes had fallen away as low-floor buses became universal, but there remained isolated pockets not within reach of passengers. Colindeep Lane in north-west London was one of them, with the 972 thus still needed all the way until 2010.

Ostensibly working a Metroline route originally operated by Thorpes, Dennis Dart SLF DP 26 (W126 WGT) at Ladbroke Grove on 3 March 2007 derives from neither; it was new to Mitcham Belle and passed to Centra, which then fell ignominiously to pieces in 2006. The buses went far and wide, and this was one subsequently to enjoy a more stable life.

Needing some refurbishment cover early in 2007, Metroline hired six ex-Metrobus East Lancs-bodied Dennis Tridents to help out at Harrow Weald garage. Coming up to Yeading on 17 February is ET 766 (LV51 YCE).

Not yet convinced that Alexander Dennis's Enviro200 was a worthy replacement for the tried and trusted Dart SLF when it came to specifying new vehicles for the 251 and 206 in 2007, Metroline ordered two batches of MAN 14.240 single-deck buses with MCV Evolution bodywork. One of them, North Wembley's MM 779 (LK07 AVL), is setting off from Arnos Grove on 8 May 2007.

Metroline also moved away from predictably sourcing Alexander Dennis double-deck products when it selected Optare Esteem-bodied Scania N230UDs for its win of the prestige 7, but was soon burned by the bodybuilder's notorious delivery delays. In order to free enough fleet-liveried buses for the 7, the company hired Tridents from neighbouring First to fill in on the 297. Both Alexander ALX400 and Plaxton President bodies were represented, and TNA 32952 (W952 ULL) at Wembley on 23 June 2007 is one of the former.

Metroline took Enviro200s after all and went on to acquire large numbers as all its competitors faltered and fell away. First up was a batch of the shortest (9m) version for the E6, shown at Greenford on 22 October 2007 by Perivale West's DES 799 (LK07 BEU).

A unique and extremely busy link across the top of Hampstead Heath, the 210 had never been double-deck, but conversion came in 2008 when it was realised that, with careful driving, its narrowest sections could be safely negotiated. TAs thus came to Cricklewood, among them TA 114 (V314 GLB) at Golders Green on 21 October 2009.

Still on Metroline's books for private hire, RML 903 (WLT 903) was the 24th and last of the 30ft Routemaster batch new in 1961. At last repainted, it is seen at Wisley airfield during the Cobham bus rally of 6 April 2008.

Attractive and imposing even if they did take forever to arrive, the SEL class of Optare Esteem-bodied Scania N230UDs accomplished their customary decade and on 24 May 2008 in Oxford Street, Perivale West's SEL 806 (LK57 KBJ) is at the beginning of it. This would end up being the last of its type in service (see page 82).

All-over ads, prolific in the 1970s but banished after 1984, roared back in the 2000s, the money from them just being too good to refuse. Despite watering down the concept by not continuing the ad round the front of the bus, Holloway's Volvo B7TL VP 507 (LK53 LYA) at Archway on 25 July 2008 is making a good fist of hustling punters to watch *Dirty Dancing* at the Aldwych Theatre.

The Enviro400 increased in number as batch after batch entered service. The TALs on the 16 out of Cricklewood had lasted longer than the two previous types to have manned that prestige route, but in 2008 they gave way to the likes of TE 908 (LK58 CNZ), seen at Victoria on 28 September.

Metroline continued to hedge its bets when it came to ordering new vehicles in 2009; though no more MANs were taken, MCV's Evolution body was also available on Enviro200s and thus came a one-off combination of ten as the DM class for route 190. They also visited the E8 from time to time, as in this Ealing Broadway capture of Brentford's DM 963 (LK09 EKL) on 27 September 2009.

The established manufacturers' early hybrid efforts weren't that successful. One of five Optare Tempo hybrids taken by Metroline for the E8 in 2009, OTH 975 (LK09 EKH), is at Ealing Broadway on 21 October.

Carved out of an irregular accessible bus service, the 205 became enormously successful, but Metroline lost it after the first contract. Before Stagecoach snapped it up, TPL 266 (LN51 KZA), temporarily of Perivale, makes a visit to the route at Liverpool Street on 19 June 2009.

With the delivery of Enviro400s for the E2 at Brentford, the Metroline blue skirt was no more, but all other companies' distinguishing features had also been banished. Drawing up to Greenford on 21 October 2009 is TE 979 (LK59 DZC), but its tenure was destined to be short-lived as Brentford would be standardised on Volvo B7TLs (VWs) when they arrived in 2010.

Suitably bland after an all-red repaint when captured at Victoria on 14 November 2009 is Willesden's VPL 170 (Y196 NLK).

Having been bought by Metroline in 2004, Armchair found its heritage overwritten, first with the loss of its identity and then with the exit of the 237's original Tridents, which were replaced by TPs dislodged from elsewhere. Metroline's renewed contract applying from 9 January 2010 specified new buses, and Volvo B9TLs were on order, but on 7 February Brentford's TP 415 (LK03 CFL) is loading up at White City.

Some tinkering was performed to the most recent extent of the 139, to get its turning buses at Waterloo into the best position to take passengers back to central London. Thus it was projected a little further along to make a U-turn opposite the Old Vic. Cricklewood's TP 427 is almost there in this shot taken on 21 April 2010.

Its flirtation with pastel shades long forgotten, Dennis Dart SLF DLD 700 (LK55 KLS) is heading south through Camden on 18 October 2010, with a King's Cross stablemate on its tail. This was a second site and thus merited a new code (KC, where its predecessor had used KX).

Metroline's second batch of MAN 14.240s followed on from a second batch of Scanias, hence their fleetnumbers in the 800s. Coming into Hatton Cross bus station on 21 March 2010 is MM 813 (LK57 AYG), currently allocated to Perivale but destined to move with the 90 to Perivale West the following year.

With steadily increasing PVRs, bus stations were starting to get crowded. The 217 and 231 at Turnpike Lane had to be shoved into the top corner, as in this 20 July 2010 shot of Potters Bar's TP 433 (LK03 GFZ).

On 19 November 2011 Edgware's Enviro400 TE 841 (LK57 AXW) stages through Harrow & Wealdstone. Busy and generally reliable, this route had been TE-operated for four years by now.

Red repaints now reached the newest members of Metroline's Volvo B7TL and Dennis Trident intake. Here in Oxford Street on 13 April 2011 is Willesden's VP 503 (LK53 LXW), from the batch of Volvo B7TLs immediately preceding the glut for the 6 and 98 but since transferred in to join them.

Also repainted and encountered in Oxford Street, VPL 592 (LK04 NNA) has broken down on 3 July 2011 and is waiting for some help. The 390 was now operated out of Holloway, the second King's Cross being unable to accommodate double-deckers.

TfL had made much of the environmentally friendly credentials of early hybrid double-deckers, emblazoning them with foliage decals irrespective of their company ownership. Subsequent deliveries, in Metroline's case Enviro400Hs, entered service in plain red, like TEH 1105 (LK60 AHV), new in November 2010 and allocated to Cricklewood two months later. It is approaching the Waterloo terminus of the 139 on 13 February 2011.

A couple of TfL contractors suffered paint quality problems, whereas others managed to retain the shine on original paint jobs for up to a decade. DLD 194 (Y264 NLK), working from Potters Bar in this East Finchley shot of 28 August 2011, was not one of them.

The solution was a repaint, which by the 2010s was accompanied by a mid-career refurbishment enabling buses to take on a second consecutive contract on an existing route or allocation to another one as fit. Perivale's DP 1015 (RL51 DOU), seen at Ladbroke Grove Sainsbury's on 8 October 2011, had been new to Armchair but kept hold of its fleetnumber into the Metroline era.

In the fight for hegemony between Alexander Dennis and Volvo, the latter had stumbled when its B7TLs developed noise problems that could only be remedied by the creation of an all-new product that would placate TfL. This was the B9TL, which with Wrightbus Gemini 2 bodywork became the VW class under Metroline. The 237's intake at Brentford were also able to work the 190 and did so frequently, as in this picture of VW 1035 (LK10 BXC) at Richmond on 7 May 2012.

Hefty Volvo B9TL orders placed in 2012 swept the existing Dennis Trident and/or Volvo B7TL stock off Holloway's 43, 134 and W7. Rounding Muswell Hill Broadway on 27 May is VW 1255 (LK12 AUX).

Throughout any modern London bus company's history, routes come and go according to the unpredictable whims of tendering. One such was the 70, awarded to First for 2012 takeup. Its loss more or less finished the careers of the Dart SLFs acquired ex-Centra; DP 26 (W126 WGT), seen pulling into Ladbroke Grove Sainsbury's on 17 June 2012, had five days left in service and was sold in July.

On 28 July 2012 Cricklewood's DE 957 (LK58 CTO) is setting off from Brent Cross. In yet another of Metroline's wholesale garage upheavals, the 326 had just been reallocated from Perivale West to Cricklewood.

A swap of vehicles effected before the 70's loss in 2012 put the outgoing DPs on that route so they could be withdrawn, with the MMs taking up service on the E6 instead. Coming up to Hayes & Harlington station on 9 June is MM 784 (LK57 EHU).

Metroline favoured the Wrightbus Gemini 2-bodied Volvo B9TL again when the 24 was won back from London General late in 2012, and here at Trafalgar Square on 25 November is Holloway's VW 1383 (LK62 DSE). Government environmental funding also allowed the purchase of a small batch of Volvo's new hybrid offering, the B5LH (known by Metroline as the VWH class), but both types would soon be ousted from the 24 when something rather more special came along.

Chapter 4

Expanding West

Competition was a noble objective, but in the real world, rivals are bought up and merged and new monopolies appear. By the 2010s the number of TfL contractors was in single figures, represented by international conglomerates, and in 2012 one of them, FirstGroup, began pulling out of London altogether. Metroline saw the opportunity to expand westward by purchasing the operations of its natural neighbour in 2013 to produce Metroline West. In broader terms, hybrids were also now standard, prices of such vehicles having fallen sufficient to obviate the need for government subsidy any more. There was also a wild card, harking back to more centrally inspired bus-operating decisions; the Wrightbus New Bus for London, or NBfL, or Borismaster.

Another mix of VWs and VWHs was specified for Metroline's retention of the busy 52. Setting off from Victoria on 24 February 2013 is Willesden's VWH 1415 (LK62 DWU). Only a subtle logo proclaims this bus's hybrid status, but the almost comically short wheelbase of the Volvo B5LH by comparison with its traditionally laid-out diesel counterparts is a dead giveaway.

The most notable development of the 2010s was the Wrightbus New Bus for London (NBfL). The 24 had the inaugural batch, exemplified at Hampstead Heath on 17 August 2013 by Holloway's LT 13 (LTZ 1013).

First's loss on 22 June 2013 was Metroline's gain, and what a gain. The new Metroline West lost no time assimilating its large fleet into company practice, and by 29 June, TE 1747 (SN09 CGG) at Ealing Broadway had already received its new fleetnumber and fleetname; up until then it had been First DN 33607.

Uxbridge garage was a little slower to peel off First's transfers and decals. Application of Metroline legal lettering (in this case to the window behind the exit door) took priority, so at least what is now DC 1553 (LK53 FDJ), a Caetano Nimbus-bodied Dennis Dart SLF seen at Uxbridge on 29 June 2013, will satisfy any examiners that care to visit.

Metroline's second route to go over to New Bus for London operation was the 390. In the absence of a memorable name (NBfL being the official abbreviation of its rather anodyne moniker), the public gave it one – Borismaster, after the colourful mayor who had driven it through in only four years since election. The vehicles themselves, all owned by TfL and leased to operators, had another code again, LT, evoking London Transport's AEC Regent type of the 1930s. At first they even had conductors, or, more accurately, Customer Assistants, hence the guarded open platform. A further eccentricity was a block of Northern Ireland plates booked to match their fleetnumbers; Holloway's LT 102 (LTZ 1102) demonstrates at Archway on 5 April 2014.

Scania's position in the race to populate London with low-floor buses had dwindled to fourth place, with some diehard loyalists for all of that. First had not been one of them, but needed buses quickly to usher out the last artics in London, which ran on the 207. Thus came 39 Polish-built integrals at the close of 2011. At White City on 17 February 2014 is Hayes's SN 1949 (YR61 RUY), previously known as SN 36061. They were non-standard at Metroline, however, and were disposed of as quickly as possible.

After a tremendously successful decade supplying the capital with its Gemini body on Volvo chassis, Wrightbus made some modifications, principally to address heat intake problems during increasingly hot summers. The upper-deck windows were thus reduced in height to produce the Gemini 3. Orders against contracts won were increasingly wholly for hybrids, and the Volvo B5LH stock taken to retain the 7 in 2014 was typical. Seen at the latter-day Oxford Circus stand of this route on 14 July 2014 is Perivale West's VWH 2019 (LK14 FBV).

Showing off its rich crop of cabbages in this 29 April 2014 shot on the periphery of Victoria is TEH 916 (LK58 CPN), one of the five pioneering Alexander Dennis Enviro400H hybrids that had been new to Cricklewood five years earlier. The succeeding E40H version competed with Volvo's B5LH for hybrid orders, with Metroline alternating between large numbers of each. A decade was got out of the original quintet, which worked from Cricklewood all their lives.

Nothing new had come to Harrow Weald since the takeover of the garage by Volvo B7TLs (VPs) in 2004, but the regaining of school route 640 ten years later required something newer, so a handful of VWs moved in. When not needed on this peak-hour service, they joined the pack of VPs on the 140, as in this Harrow shot of VW 1245 (LK12 AAN) on 9 September 2014.

All-over ads weren't just for bringing in extra revenue (though that they did!). Sombre occasions like Remembrance Sunday developed their own culture, with buses liveried in symbolic poppies for the period leading up to the commemoration held on the Sunday nearest 11 November every year. 2014's iteration is shown on Cricklewood's inaugural hybrid TEH 915 (SN08 AAO) at Oxford Circus that 3 December.

Another large batch of Wrightbus Gemini 3-bodied Volvo B5LHs was ordered for Metroline's win of routes 34 and 125 at the tail end of 2004. Allocated to Potters Bar, VWH 2024 (LK64 EDC) is departing Arnos Grove on 27 November of that year.

The 112's new stock from the end of October 2014 comprised ten 10.8m E20Ds, and on 15 April 2015, Cricklewood's DEL 2067 (LK64 ECV) is seen coming up to Ealing Broadway. Plans were being hatched to amend the final section of the route so that it would approach this point from the opposite direction.

Metroline's performance on the W9 was deemed satisfactory enough to warrant a two-year extension. During this period the road layout at Enfield Town had been changed so that the carriageways shifted over by one. On the new southbound bore on 19 December 2015 is Potters Bar's DEM 1347 (LK62 DFF).

On 15 April 2015 Uxbridge's DE 1812 (YX10 BGE) has just left Hayes & Harlington station and will turn at the next junction. The route was about to be renewed for another period with Metroline West, but structural changes soon after would transform this outlying service into a double-deck route.

The SEL-class Scanias normally to be found on the 297 at Perivale West often appeared on the 90, as seen in this Hayes & Harlington station shot of 8 April 2015 by SEL 750 (LK07 BBO), with a mid-life repaint that had removed Metroline's traditional blue skirt.

The Borismaster lent itself ideally to the application of all-over ads, and literally thousands of them followed to the present day. One of the most significant, and certainly the longest lasting, was that for Fender's anniversary Stratocaster guitar, applied to Holloway's LT 100 (LTZ 1100). It is seen at King's Cross on 27 May 2015.

Less common by far were rear ads on single-deckers, but these were usually tailored to local businesses and attractions. Parkside Studio College in Hayes was guaranteed to see a throughput of Uxbridge-operated buses, so paid for an ad on the back of DE 1810 (YX10 BFY), which is setting off from its home base on 16 July 2015.

Even with relatively little choice in modern bus designs, operators remained broadly loyal to one manufacturer or another. Having built up a large fleet of Alexander Dennis Enviro400s and its E40H hybrid development, Metroline progressed on to the MMC in 2015, but bought only the one batch and never touched an ADL double-decker again. Operating past Edgware Road Bakerloo Underground station on 10 October is Cricklewood's TEH 2072 (LK15 CWA).

Volvo had won the battle for Metroline orders, and batch after batch of Wrightbus Gemini 3-bodied B5LH hybrids characterised the mid-2010s. The 6 and 98, as the company's flagship routes, often co-opted new buses meant for lesser contracts, but these particular examples were taken on their own merit, to replace the 04-reg VPs that had seen off the Routemasters in 2004. Here in the Edgware Road on 15 October 2015 is Willesden's VWH 2107 (LK15 CXF).

Another batch of DELs took over the 331 at the close of 2015. Uxbridge's DEL 2145 (LK65 EAA) is at the beginning of this route, which snakes out of Greater London, explores some pretty and leafy territory to be found immediately beyond, and then dips back in to reach Ruislip.

Most central London routes were cleared for Borismasters as the TfL-owned vehicles arrived. Notably excluded were the 6 and 98, but the 16 up the straight of the Edgware Road was fair game and received examples in the autumn of 2015. Here on its way south on 15 October is Cricklewood's LT 558 (LTZ 1558). A second batch into that garage would convert the 168 not long after.

LT 543 (LTZ 1543) at Waterloo on 16 December 2015 was actually one of the 16's batch of Borismasters, but Cricklewood gained some more six weeks after that route's conversion. A third batch would take over the 189 in the summer of 2016, providing a large pool from which to draw. Even so, the 168 would be subjected to multiple transfers later in the decade, which would see its own batch moved with it.

Wrightbus's redesign of its Gemini 3 body in 2015 didn't actually merit a new model name, so in its absence the enthusiast fraternity made up its own, some of them unprintable. Willesden Junction received some on Volvo B5LH chassis to take over the 295 for Metroline West, and here at Fulham Broadway on 9 November 2015 is VWH 2123 (LK65 EAY).

The 324 passed from Sovereign to Metroline on 24 October 2015, using Enviro200s from Cricklewood. Leaving Brent Cross on a sunny 11 September 2016 is DE 1027 (LK59 AVP).

A bureaucratic mix-up saw the order of new buses that were too long for their intended route 487, meaning that this route had to see out the entirety of its renewed Metroline contract with its existing Enviro200s. One of them is Alperton's DE 1668 (YX09 AEY), seen pulling into South Harrow bus station on 13 May 2016.

Dual-sourcing is one thing, but when it conflicts with the orderly replacement of superannuated buses, some garages end up having to take unfamiliar types. Volvo B7TLs thus appeared at Uxbridge, hitherto a Dennis Trident and Enviro400 operator. On 13 May 2016 VP 479 (LK03 GLJ) is setting off from Uxbridge station on the U4.

Another all-over ad on a Borismaster is on Holloway's LT 12 (LTZ 1012, ex-LK13 FJF) at Trafalgar Square on 26 May 2016. It was sponsored by Pepe Jeans between April and July.

Blithely operating through Alperton on 13 May 2016, Perivale West's Scania SEL 755 (LK07 BCE) would no longer be able to work on the 79 after 6 August, when this route was reallocated to Perivale.

To make room at Alperton for the introduction of new route 483 on 10 September 2016, the 245 had to leave. It took its Volvo B5LHs along with it to Perivale, and one such is VW 1377 (LK62 DOH), seen loading up at Golders Green on the 11th.

The 223 out of Alperton was performing satisfactorily enough in this 10 April 2016 Harrow shot of DEM 1917 (YX61 EKY) to be rewarded with two extra years, which began on 15 October.

Cricklewood's third batch of Borismasters accomplished the conversion of the 189 from 30 June 2016. However, the earlier contingents could now spread their wings, and this one, seen departing Brent Cross on 11 September, is LT 648 (LTZ 1648), taken for the 168 the previous December. Its roundel badge has already gone missing, for all we know onto a chain around someone's neck.

With the important 114 coming into Uxbridge as a new contract, two lesser routes were pushed out to Hayes. One was the U5, seen in the hands of DE 1896 (YX60 BZB) on 11 September 2016. In this Uxbridge station capture it is displaying its new garage code in the customary side position, plus a windscreen card.

The 114 terminated at Ruislip, closer to Harrow Weald garage than Uxbridge, but the former was full and it was therefore assumed as a Metroline West contract. Wrightbus Gemini 3-bodied Volvo B5LHs were now the company's de facto standard and increasing in number, and on 11 September 2016 VWH 2181 (LK16 DGE) is on its way west towards Harrow bus station.

Coming the other way on 11 September 2016 is Alperton's Volvo B9TL VW 1755 (LK59 CWR), introducing the most useful new link that came with the 483, which could so easily otherwise have been just a sectionalisation of the 83's southern part. This it was, but TfL recognised its potential as a lateral link across north-west London.

The Scania N230UDs acquired from First were discarded when the loss of the 427 to Abellio on 8 April 2017 was made good by transferring its VWs to the 207. Prior to that, Hayes's SN 1945 (YR61 RUO) is getting under way at Shepherd's Bush on 21 February 2016.

A little on the ungainly side, the five BYD electric double-deckers taken by Metroline on an experimental basis were allocated to the 98 at Willesden from May 2016. On 18 July 2017 BYD 1473 (LJ16 EZO), replete with TfL's cheerful leaf graphics publicising reduced-emission buses, is rounding Marble Arch.

Electric propulsion was at last approaching cost-effectiveness on a general roll-out scale, but there were also workarounds like stop-start engine operation, as seen in contemporary cars. The ADL E20D MMCs taken for the 235 in 2017 were so fitted, though from personal experience, the ensuing bruising shudders meant that the format was not adopted on subsequent diesel buses. Coming into Hounslow on 3 June 2017 is Brentford's DEL 2248 (LK66 FSF).

Expanding West

The peculiar backlash against perceived hordes of under-used buses in the Oxford Street corridor, combined with a frankly crazy desire to pedestrianise this critical thoroughfare, caused TfL to begin gutting through routes towards the end of the decade. The proposed total withdrawal of trunk route 13 met with such outrage that a compromise solution was effected. It ended up adopting the 82's contract (awarded to Tower Transit) under its own number. Prior to that, Metroline's Enviro400 TE 911 (LK58 COJ) of Potters Bar is at Marble Arch on its way to Victoria.

The work lost by Potters Bar when the 82 was withdrawn was remedied by reallocating the 134 from Holloway and thus restoring the situation prior to 1983, although the route had been pruned repeatedly at its northern extent in the intervening years. Heading south past Warren Street on 11 November 2017 is TE 1423 (LK62 DXT).

The 6 was also pulled out of its traditional routeing along Oxford Street and Regent Street, but its diversion via Park Lane and Piccadilly opened up a useful new link not operated hitherto. Before that was implemented, Willesden's VWH 2112 (LK15 CXM) is making the turn at Oxford Circus, which now sports an X-shaped multi-directional pedestrian crossing of a style common in Japan.

Now transferred from the 427 to the 207 is Volvo B9TL VW 1822 (BV10 WVT), leaving White City on 13 August 2017. It wouldn't have long to get too comfortable, however, as the whims of tendering soon saw this route lost to Abellio as well.

When introduced in 1990, express route 607 demanded something a little more special than the average bus; its second and third generations of buses were fitted with coach seats, but the fourth just comprised standard First VNLs and the fifth mixed two batches of buses unwanted elsewhere (Enviro400s and Volvo B7TLs). With heavy mileage on this limited-stop service, the buses were worked much harder than their stop-start contemporaries, and in this Ealing Broadway shot of 12 April 2017, Uxbridge's Volvo B7TL VW 1570 (LK55 ABF) is already looking tired.

Exemplifying the Carnival-only double-deck roster on the 316 is Cricklewood's TE 723 (LK56 FHT) at the junction of Harrow Road with Elgin Avenue on 28 August 2017. The extension in the modern era to White City had made double-deck operation even more necessary, but locals along this final stretch wouldn't budge.

After a decade with Scanias, the 7 was kept hold of by Metroline and refreshed in 2017 with new Volvo B5LHs like Perivale's VWH 2288 (LK17 CYT), seen at Oxford Circus on 6 December. This was another route to be stripped out of a section of Oxford Street; its old leg onward to Tottenham Court Road and the British Museum was appended to a rerouteing of the 10, which itself was withdrawn a year later.

Once the major carrier southwestward towards Staines, the 117 had been localised in 1978 and, in the tendering era, had fallen subject to a long line of less-than-satisfactory operators. Closer to the present, it found itself passing from one local firm to the next whenever its contract came up, and in 2017 it was Metroline's turn, Brentford stepping up with Enviro200s including DE 1000 (LK09 EOB) at Hounslow on 3 July 2017. This contract too would only be a one-off, with London United having the 117 next.

On 6 January 2017 Willesden's Volvo B5LH VWH 2120 (LK15 CXV) is setting off from Victoria. This was one of the 6 and 98's motors, but the 52 would be due its own VWHs shortly.

Borismaster LT 190 (LTZ 1190) was new in this smart silver livery, and on 14 January 2018 is carrying it past futuristic new construction at the 16's Victoria end. The bus was now operating out of Cricklewood after three years at Holloway, but in 2019 would go home.

Historically a bonded pair differing only at their ends, the 28 and 31 had been separated in 1999 and their fortunes had since diverged. Metroline won the 31 from Tower Transit in 2018 and equipped it with Volvo B9TLs (VWs) until orders for new Volvo B5LHs (VMHs) could be firmed up. Taking the right turn from Notting Hill Gate towards its latter-day White City objective, rather than proceeding onward towards its former terminus at Chelsea, is Perivale West's VW 1190 (LK11 CYA) on 3 June 2019.

Route branding would seem an obvious strategy for hustling passengers, but in London it has always fallen flat due to the high likelihood that buses so treated would be put out on the wrong routes. The solution adopted by TfL when it tried out the concept again in 2017 was to ask for only a proportion of the selected routes' buses to receive the appropriate vinyl embellishments, which were colour-coded per route. Here at Uxbridge on 22 May 2018 is DE 1585 (LK08 FNH), but the scheme didn't manage to mask deeper structural problems and soon faded away.

While the market for van-based minibuses was erased overnight by the Dennis Mini Dart SLF, the need still existed for buses of a width narrow enough to serve backstreets into areas that would otherwise be isolated. The Optare Solo Slimline was the best option if operators didn't want to resort to van conversions, and it was still around when the H2 changed hands, Arriva London South's 2006-vintage examples giving way to the updated SR version when Metroline took over in 2018. At Golders Green on 22 September 2019 is OS 2504 (YJ68 FXG), unusually with LED blinds as TfL's rollers didn't fit.

When tendering began changing the fates of London buses, the 268 was one of the first routes to leave, passing from Cricklewood to London Country in 1986. A generation later, after a host of operators good, bad and indifferent, it was restored to Cricklewood as a Metroline contract. Golders Green bus station was so full that the 268 was consigned to squatting in a corner, as DE 1117 (LK10 BYD) is doing on 11 August 2018. A repaint has unfortunately wiped out every instance of this Enviro200's black trim, an irritating habit that Metroline would only go on to ramp up.

The accelerating pace of service cuts as passenger numbers ebbed away from London's buses messed up the hitherto orderly allocations of buses to the PVRs specified when their most recent contracts had been firmed up. The drift of Borismasters away from their original pitches was thus all the more conspicuous, with the 32 the most recent posting for Cricklewood examples to visit. LT 548 (LTZ 1548) is leaving Edgware on 31 August 2018, though the following day would see the 32 reallocated to Edgware garage, which fielded no Borismasters.

Brand loyalty (see page 64) was a two-way street, and when family drama at Wrightbus both jeopardised delivery times and threatened to tank the manufacturer altogether, Metroline grew annoyed enough to switch its preference for Volvo B5LH bodying to MCV, which manufactured the relatively conservative EvoSeti design in Egypt. Taken for the win of the 30 and the welcome double-decking of the 274 in 2018, the resulting VMH class is exemplified at Baker Street on 1 July of that year by King's Cross's VMH 2462 (LK18 AKZ).

After seven years with Tower Transit (originally First) and two decades before that with Stagecoach East London and its predecessors, the 30 was won by Metroline in 2018 and put into King's Cross. Heading west along Balls Pond Road towards Highbury Corner on 8 July is VMH 2467 (LK18 AMV).

The 113 at Edgware was also in line for VMH conversion, upgrading from its previous spread of 60-reg TEs and TEHs, and on 16 November 2018 in Oxford Street we see VMH 2446 (LK18 AGV).

On the afternoon of 5 May 2018 LT 745 (LTZ 1745), in an all-over advert livery for Nike, finds itself south of Waterloo. The 168 was now based out of Holloway, and this garage had even more routes from which to pool Borismasters; this particular one was of a batch new to the the 91.

The electric revolution was now upon us, and the hesitance of both British manufacturing industry and the financially cautious London bus operators to comply with the politically-inspired dogma that mandated the introduction of such buses allowed the Chinese in by the back door. Alexander Dennis's tie-up with BYD saw the former's existing Enviro200 body now adorning the latter's D8UR chassis and, with no competition yet evident, large numbers ensued across all TfL operators. Manning a 46 at Hampstead on 21 October 2018 is Holloway's BEL 2520 (LJ18 FHT).

On 31 August 2018 Edgware's Enviro400 TE 1100 (LK60 AHL) is approaching its home base as if nothing is amiss, but the need to balance work at Alperton following the loss of that garage's 223 and 224 to Sovereign on 13 October saw the route reallocated there on that day. More complicatedly, Alperton had never operated Enviro400s and these buses, coming across with the 204, would be its first.

On 8 September 2019 at Muswell Hill, Potters Bar's DE 1169 (LK11 DXB) is adding a little extra capacity to the 234, which was normally operated by shorter DEMs. It had come here from King's Cross in March, following the loss of the 214 to London General, and would stay until mid-July 2020.

It seemed that Metroline made the same mistake repeatedly when it came to specifying buses for tenders it had won. Having already had to redeploy the buses it had realised were too long for their intended 487, it now had to reorder in the same manner for the 393 and reallocate the DELs purchased in error. Until the new DEMs were delivered, Holloway even had to hire the buses used by the 393's previous operator, Arriva London North. With a correct garage code at least but still sporting Arriva logos, ENS 4 (LJ07 EDP) is coming up to Highbury Corner on 30 June 2019.

Although terminating at the bus station within its grounds, the 81 left Hounslow garage after Metroline took it over from London United on 27 July 2019. A new garage at Spring Grove, Lampton, was opened to operate it, with 13 Volvo B9TLs transferred from Harrow Weald and six from Perivale West. As evinced by the garage code still in situ, VW 1382 (LK62 DRZ), seen getting going on 29 July, was one of the latter.

Expanding West

In the time-honoured manner, any bus type gradually makes way for newer ones, with route tendering generally driving the process. The 274 was double-decked in 2018 and passed its Enviro200s (DEs) to the 214, replacing its tired-out 2005-vintage Dart SLFs (DLDs). DE 1323 (LK12 AXG) is now in charge in this 5 April 2019 shot at Camden. However, this route had already been lost on tender to London General and would depart on 17 August. DE 1323 would find itself transferred to Greenford to replace an older counterpart.

Electric double-deck buses were the logical progression of the format, the issues with weight and battery distribution having largely been addressed (if not wholly solved, as was also the case with overall range). Once again BYD had almost total control of the market, with its D8UR-DD chassis bodied by Alexander Dennis alone with a variant of the Enviro400 City body. Coming across (in fact around) the heavily revamped Old Street junction on the afternoon of 12 September 2019 is Holloway's BDE 2616 (LJ19 CUA).

Optare had long had a double-deck integral in the making, and was able to adapt its MetroCity to electric propulsion in time to take on BYD. Three London operators ordered examples of the resulting MetroCity EV, but delivery times let the company down; the 30 for the 134 at Metroline's Potters Bar took nearly a year all to be in place, even before COVID, and no further orders have been placed. On 8 September 2019 OME 2657 (YJ19 HVH) is climbing towards Muswell Hill.

Metroline's relatively untroubled tenure on the 209 was thrown into disarray in 2019 when Hammersmith Bridge was declared off limits to everything; even pedestrians. TfL scrambled to maintain the link with an Underground station by diverting the route to Putney Bridge, but when this threatened to become permanent, a new link was created to that point. The 378 was operated off half the 209's schedule before both were transferred on tender to London General, and during that spell, Brentford's DE 1010 (LK09 ENM) is seen at Barnes Pond on 12 August 2019.

Only the first three years of the 1987-introduced H13 had been spent under what became Metroline; since then, Sovereign had been in charge. However, in 2019 it was won by Metroline and allocated to Uxbridge garage of Metroline West. At the far north-west quadrant of the map on 18 September of that year is DE 1801 (YX10 BFJ).

Enormously long by modern standards, the 140 was finally split in two late in 2019 and its stopping service between Hayes & Harlington and Heathrow Airport incorporated into new Abellio-operated route 278. Far more significant was the introduction of the X140, a new service over limited stops of the old entirety, using Harrow Weald VWHs on a short-term contract. Arriving at Heathrow on 10 December 2019 is VWH 2241 (LK66 EOL).

Expanding West

Tendered and retained by Metroline West, the 607 was designated to receive new VMHs, ending the careers of the 55-reg Volvo B7TLs inherited from First Capital and subsequently brought to Uxbridge. Still carrying the branding applied in 2017 is VW 1569 (LK55 AAZ), coming into the town centre on 1 April 2019.

2019 marked the end of an era in that both major inaugural low-floor double-deck chassis reached the end of their cumulative two decades in service. Metroline's last Dennis Tridents, the final batch of Alexander ALX400-bodied TAs new to the 266 in 2005, had undergone a protracted decline over several years, still based at Cricklewood but latterly on the 210. TA 642 (LK05 GFZ) was one of the last pair to survive, and on 26 May 2019 is seen at the foot of Highgate Hill near Archway.

Volvo B7TL VP 614 (LK04 UWW) was an even more spectacular holdout, staying doggedly put on Harrow Weald's 140 for two years after the route was otherwise converted to VWHs. As the last example of its type in the company, it was given a gala send-off on 23 December 2019 and at the close of that day, has reached the 140's curtailed southern terminus at Hayes & Harlington station.

Chapter 5

Discarding Diesel

The turnover of London bus generations has become faster and faster in the modern era, all of it dictated by contracts and their whims. No more a two-decade career or even more; buses now can count themselves lucky if they complete two contract terms in a row plus one or two additional two-year spells, adding up to 14 years in total. Thus did the turn-of-the-century generation of early low-floor double-deckers produced between 1998 and 2006 come to the end of the line by 2019–20. Their contemporary low-floor single-deck counterparts, mostly Dennis Dart SLFs, made their exit at the same time.

At the time of writing, it is now the hybrids of the 2010s that are starting to grow long in the tooth. Replacing them are pure electric buses, given that hydrogen has proven something of a non-starter. In operational terms, passenger numbers were already falling during this decade, as personalised taxi services like Uber conspired with the rise of remote working to leave buses empty, particularly in central London. Then came COVID-19, which almost blew all of it apart. The struggle to recover from the virus's effects on world economies will be what characterises the next years of London bus companies, Metroline among them.

Though in a distant fourth place overall behind the Dennis Trident, Volvo B7TL and DAF DB250RS(LF), the Scania N94UD and its later N230UD development had also played its part in the history of first-generation low-floor double-deckers, and at the beginning of 2020 Metroline ushered out its last SELs. Seen at Ealing Broadway on 29 July 2019, Perivale West's SEL 806 (LK57 KBJ) was the last one in service.

Straightforward and little altered since its introduction at the end of 1968, the 282 had gone from single-deck to double-deck twice each over its lifetime, and on 7 March 2020 began a new contract with Metroline West that compelled its existing TEs to give way to hybrid TEHs. Six days before that, TE 1744 (SN09 CFZ) is captured near its Greenford garage base.

Discarding Diesel

Unable ever to work the 393 for which they had been bought in error, MMC DELs 2597–2612 found a home at Cricklewood on the 112, though their 65-reg predecessors held in place to work the 316 instead. On stand at Brent Cross on 20 July 2020 is DEL 2608 (YX19 OVM), just before the route's extension to North Finchley.

The onslaught of COVID-19 forced TfL not only to let buses run free of charge until cab doors could be sealed off, but also order the temporary double-decking of some routes for social distancing. The 112 thus benefited for a while, with TE 1090 (LK60 AGO) seen next to Cricklewood stablemate TEH 1106 (LK60 AHX) on 20 July 2020 at Brent Cross.

Suprisingly hard to bag, the lone short-wheelbase Borismaster, ST 812 (LTZ 1812), is seen on its normal route, Holloway's 91, at Trafalgar Square on 13 September 2020. This was a particularly lucky break, as not only was the 91 subsequently compelled to give up its LTs and ST due to clearance problems, but this bus was damaged in a collision at King's Cross on Boxing Day 2022 and would not return to service until 2024.

The small DM class came to the end of the line in 2021. Drawing up to Hammersmith, the mid-point of the 190, on 25 May 2020, is Brentford's DM 967 (LK58 CSF). DEs took these buses' place before DELs settled in.

After 14 years based at Edgware, the 186 was reallocated back to Harrow Weald on 1 September 2018 and converted from TE to VW operation. Here in Wealdstone High Street on 20 July 2020 is VW 1283 (LK12 AOA).

Another solid TE route, the 210, began seeing VWHs as examples made redundant from Potters Bar trickled into Cricklewood. Approaching Finsbury Park on 24 August 2020 is VWH 2038 (LK64 EHF).

Eleven VWHs put into action at Brentford when Metroline took over the 306 on 12 December 2020 were second-hand, having spent six years at Tower Transit on the 212 before that route's loss to London General. The former VH 38105 thus became VWH 2700 (BL64 MHK), and is seen at Hammersmith on Metroline's first day in charge.

COVID wasn't the only menace threatening to rip the guts out of London's bus operations. The process was already well along, with central London routes suffering enormous frequency reductions and thus releasing buses to pop up elsewhere. Cuts to the 134 at Potters Bar thus enabled some of its OME-class Optare MetroDecker EVs to turn up on the outermost 317 route, with OME 2680 (YJ69 DGE) doing just that at Enfield on 24 April 2021. It didn't help the overall situation when two of this bus's stablemates were destroyed in a battery fire at Potters Bar garage on 22 May 2022.

Another batch of second-hand buses ex-Tower Transit were used only as long as they were needed, but provided excitement in that they donned the second of what would be four identities carried in their short lives hitherto. The 328's movement from Tower Transit to Metroline at Cricklewood brought its existing Volvo B5LHs along, with VWH 2729 (BU16 UXD), formerly VH 38113, seen at Golders Green on 17 July 2021. When later loaned to Stagecoach, this bus was known as 80113, and the latter company's subsequent takeover of Tower Transit rechristened it 13123!

The wave of cuts wasn't just to frequencies, which were largely imperceptible to the public; physical sections of routes were now having to be abandoned. In the case of the 384, Hertfordshire County Council pleaded poverty in its continued ability to support the 292's section beyond London, so to allow this to be reduced, TfL extended the 384 to Edgware from Barnet but could only make it work by straightening out its legendary kinks. Seen at the Cockfosters end on 31 July 2021 is DEM 1913 (YX61 EKT), a former First example once called DM 44203.

Gradually, most of the E-routes had assumed double-deck operation, the E9 going over upon the commencement of its Abellio contract of 2016. It remained so when taken over by to Metroline West on 29 May 2021, with Greenford fielding TEs, but from the outset the garage could use its own Volvo B5LHs and did so often. Here on the western edge of Greenford, where the road opens up sufficient to permit nearside shots, is VMH 2566 (LA68 DXB) on the first day.

Brentford's 60-reg Volvo B9TL fleet had reached its second decade in service by the time of this shot of VW 1061 (LK60 AEF) at Ealing Broadway on 24 April 2021.

Barnes Bridge, behind Brentford's DE 1011 (LK09 ENN) still worked (albeit for rail only), but as of this 24 July 2021 photo the 533's objective upriver was in a hopeless state, with not even pedestrians permitted to cross Hammersmith Bridge. The 533 thus took the long way round, crossing Chiswick Bridge non-stop. In 2022 it was converted to DEL operation and in the same year was taken over by London General.

After London Transport – Metroline

Hydrogen tried as hard as it could to be a major competitor to electricity when it came to powering the next generation of London buses, but ended up falling short. Although the 7 at Perivale re-equipped with Wrightbus's Streetdeck Hydroliner model, one of which is WHD 2709 (LK70 AZT) in Oxford Street on 3 December 2021, the fuel was subject to shortages, which often took the entire batch off the road at once. To add insult to injury, the 7's frequency was chopped down severely, meaning some of the WHDs had to slum it on the far less prestigious 245 in north-west London.

The Enviro400 and E40H hybrids had a plethora of grilles at the rear, hiding various fans and systems, but in their original condition, black trim masked their awkward lines. Then came mid-life refurbishment, with its attendant repaint, and the likes of Cricklewood's TEH 1108 (LK60 AHZ), seen at Golders Green on 17 July 2021, suddenly looked awfully exposed.

Traditionally operated by Edgware, the 292 had bounced back and forth between that garage (latterly of Metroline) and Sovereign, which later occupied the garage premises itself while Metroline buses huddled outside. In 2018 it returned to Metroline with a number of Volvo B9TLs, but on 2 September 2021 was reallocated to Harrow Weald. Three days later, VW 1201 (LK11 CYV) is in Edgware, now some distance from its new base.

Since coming back to Metroline in 2018, the 231 had put out more or less whatever Potters Bar had lying around, but with a general drift towards Volvo B9TL operation as time progressed. On 24 April 2021 VW 1196 (LK11 CYO) is heading west through Enfield Town.

Borismaster operation was defeated on two original routes by roundabouts at their termini. Thus had London General's 88 already lost its LTs, and in 2021 so followed the 91, whose Holloway-based examples struggled to turn at Crouch End. Instead, it made use of VWHs swapped with the 17, plus MCV-bodied VMHs that were already pooled with the allocation at King's Cross garage. Pausing at the station of that name on 3 December 2021 is VMH 2449 (LK18 AGZ).

The orderly allocation of BDE-class BYD D8UR DD electrics to the 43 was disrupted when cuts clipped six buses off its PVR on 28 August 2021. The buses made redundant joined forces with the 91's old Borismasters on the 17, producing a messy mix of propulsion types that at least was slightly more modern than this route's previous mid-career VWH complement. King's Cross on 3 December 2021 is also the locstion of BDE 2648 (LJ19 CVY).

The loss of the 235 to London United in the first week of 2022 freed its MMC DELs for new work. At first they stayed put at Brentford to take over that garage's existing 190 and 533 from their previous DEs, but this shot of DEL 2261 (LK66 FTA) at Hammersmith on 12 May 2022 was only temporary, as the route had just been awarded to London General for takeover in the autumn.

On 5 March 2022 the 31 was reallocated from Perivale West to Willesden Junction, taking with it a quantity of VMHs. One was VMH 2555 (LA68 DXO), caught at the route's modern-day White City extremity on the 19th. The route has since migrated again, and at the time of writing finds itself operated out of Holloway.

Perivale West's closure saw the 297 reallocated to the original Perivale, but VMH 2583 (LF19 FXH) passed to Brentford with the 90. However, that route moved again on 17 September 2022, taking up at Perivale, meaning that this bus could now operate on the 297, as in this Ealing Broadway shot of 4 November 2022.

With the 332's gradual conversion to Borismaster following the making available of Borismasters displaced by system-wide cuts, its 2015-vintage MMC TEs moved over to the 139, and on 6 December 2022 TEH 2086 (LK15 CUG) is captured rounding the old Bullring roundabout at Waterloo, long since host to the iconic IMAX.

Spring Grove garage added the 120 on 8 January 2022, allowing both its VWHs ex-Perivale West to wander to the 81 and VWs from the latter to return the favour, as VW 1386 (LK62 DTN) is doing in this Hounslow shot of 12 June 2022.

The 168 made its third reallocation since becoming operated by Metroline, passing from Cricklewood back to Holloway on 1 May 2021. On 4 November 2022, Borismaster LT 662 (LTZ 1662) is rounding St George's Circus on its way to Elephant & Castle and the useful terminus beyond. However, plans had now been hatched to withdraw the 168 and append it to the moribund 1, which were implemented in the autumn of 2023.

After London Transport – Metroline

The 533's departure for London General allowed half the 66-reg MMC E20D batch to move on from Brentford. DEL 2261 (LK66 FTA) was transferred to Willesden Junction, which began operating the 316 at the start of 2023 as a reallocation from Cricklewood, and on 29 June 2023 it is seen at White City.

Some truly brutal cuts were threatened in central London if the Mayor couldn't secure subsidy from an increasingly unwilling central government. Though moneys were ultimately found to save the majority of the routes at risk, one withdrawal did slip through. Trolleybus replacement route 271 had been in being since 1961, and it seemed that the inconvenience of its stand at Highgate Village was enough to doom it, with three local routes clumsily diverted to cover it. Holloway's VWH 2098 (LK15 CWW) is nearing Archway on 26 January 2023, a week before its end.

When new in 1989, the 234 reached Archway as a localisation of trunk route 134's top end, but over the years it fell back to the north and succumbed to minibuses. To offset the 271's withdrawal in 2023, it was extended from its most recent terminus at Highgate Wood back to Archway, and on 5 September DEM 1337 (LK62 DAA), transferred with the 234 to Holloway to fill the gap left by the 271, is in Barnet High Street.

New buses deployed to central London invariably drift off the front line in their later careers, and the Borismasters, for all their unique prestige status, were no exception. In their case, cuts removed their raison d'être in town, and LT 102 (LTZ 1102), no longer needed when the 390 lost a third of its runout, was refurbished for a quieter career on the H91, taken over by Metroline on 4 March 2023. On 7 September it is setting off from Hounslow West, sporting not just a second fleetname on the front but two yellow diamond stickers announcing its hybrid propulsion to the Fire Brigade.

In a similar situation to when the 13 replaced the 82, the proper 16, once a powerhouse fielding over sixty buses, was withdrawn in its current format in 2023 but its prestige number used to rechristen the 332. This inadvertently restored the 16 number to the Neasden terminus it had been compelled to vacate in 1997, in a previous upheaval of Cricklewood-operated routes. On 27 April 2023, the 332 on its penultimate day is in the hands of Cos-liveried LT 804 (LTZ 1804), which is making the turn towards Paddington that the revamped 16 would be doing from the 29th.

One concept that Boris Johnson had promised in his time as Mayor but never got around to implementing was picked up by Sadiq Khan in 2023. This was Superloop, a new identity for a wheel of orbital express buses that would hopefully bring extra services to the suburbs at the same time as they were being stripped out of central London. The first conversion, to split hairs, wasn't actually a loop but a renumbering of established route 607. Its Greenford-based VMHs like VMH 2566 (LA68 DXB) at the new SL8's White City start point on 15 July, its first day, donned this smart new livery.

Metroline took a second batch of BYD D8UR-DD electric double-deckers against its renewed contract for the 204, though it was discovered as they arrived that there were clearance problems on that route. Instead they took over the 142, regained from Sovereign at the same time, and that route's WDE order was put on the 204. On 5 September 2023 Edgware's BDE 2763 (LG22 AXU), with the new standard electronic blind box, is about to turn right towards Bushey and Watford.

Horribly 'tomatoed', the disparaging enthusiast term applying to the kind of repaint that erased from the MMC bodystyle of E20D every single item of black trim, DEL 2250 (LK66 FSJ) emerges from its new home at Edgware, which took over the 251 from Sovereign on 2 September 2023. In physical terms, the move was actually from one side to another of the same garage site shared with Metroline's RATP-owned neighbour.

Another routine repaint was less conspicuous, though by comparison with the top picture on page 74, Holloway-based Borismaster LT 190 (LTZ 1190) has lost its individuality. Seen on 7 April 2023 at Waterloo, it is also about to lose the chance to operate on the 168, which would be withdrawn on 30 September.

Chapter 6

The Future

With an eye to a gradually firming target of 2030 for the replacement by TfL of all diesel buses, contracts have been awarded according to the propulsion type tendered for by the operator ultimately dubbed victorious. Electrics and hydrogen (though none of the latter have been specified in some time) garner the full seven years, with hybrids six and diesels four or five, all of the latter two categories timed to end in 2030 so that, unlike the situation that saw step-entrance buses serve unremuneratively short lifespans up to 2005, will at least fulfil their remaining book value.

On 21 September 2024 the 210 will begin another term with Metroline, and a seven-year one due to being restocked with electric double-deckers yet to be determined. The revamped Archway junction is the location of this 7 April 2023 shot of Cricklewood's VW 1829 (BF10 LSO), an originally First London Volvo B9TL (VN 37877) that had crossed the intra-Metroline line in 2019 and gone on to operate out of a host of garages. At the time of compilation of this book it had since transferred to Greenford, in fact its original home.

In August 2023 the 206 was announced as awarded to and retained by Metroline West, though with new electric buses. Its long-wheelbase E20Ds will have completed two contract terms by then, the first having been novated from First London in mid-stream. This bus itself, Willesden Junction's DEL 1973 (YX12 AFK), seen at Harlesden on 12 June 2021, was thus new as DMV 44305, but has only ever worked this route.

Other books you might like:

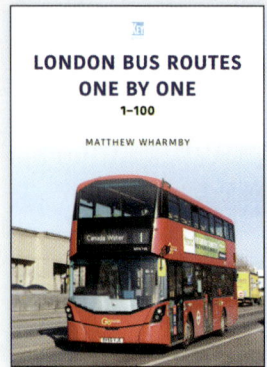

Transport Systems Series, Vol. 3

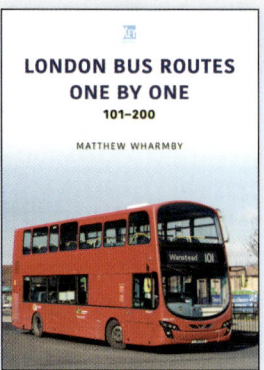

Transport Systems Series, Vol. 4

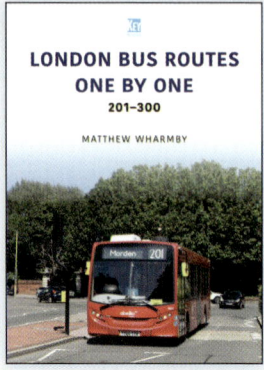

Transport Systems Series, Vol. 5

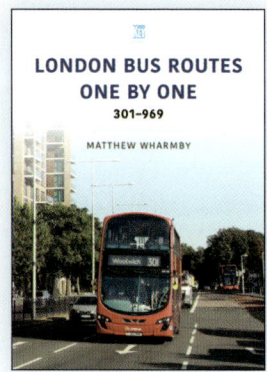

Transport Systems Series, Vol. 6

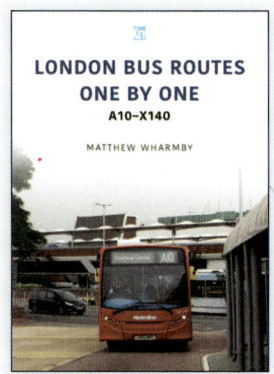

Transport Systems Series, Vol. 7

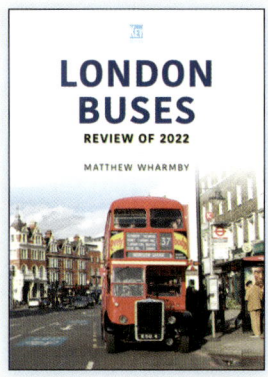

Transport Systems Series, Vol. 8

For our full range of titles please visit:
shop.keypublishing.com/books

VIP Book Club

Sign up today and receive
TWO FREE E-BOOKS

Be the first to find out about our forthcoming book releases and receive exclusive offers.

Register now at **keypublishing.com/vip-book-club**

Our VIP Book Club is a 100% spam-free zone, and we will never share your email with anyone else.
You can read our full privacy policy at: privacy.keypublishing.com